Contents

Spotted hyenas

Zebras

What are hyenas?

Hyenas look like dogs, but are not related to them. They are fierce **carnivores** that hunt and **scavenge** food, mainly at night. Most live in groups, except the aardwolf, which lives on its own.

There are four different **species** of hyena. Each species can be recognised by the pattern and length of its fur. The spotted hyena is the biggest species. The aardwolf is the smallest.

X-Ray Vision

Hold the next page up to the light to see the skeleton of a spotted hyena.

See what's inside

Spotted hyena

Brown hyena

Aardwolf

Striped hyena

Hyenas live in **savanna** (dry grassland) regions of Africa. The small maps of Africa show where each species lives. The striped hyena is also found in Asia.

Scary Creatures
HYENAS

HAU

Written by
John Malam

Created and designed
by David Salariya

BOOK   HOUSE

Author:

John Malam studied ancient history and archaeology at the University of Birmingham, England, after which he worked as an archaeologist at the Ironbridge Gorge Museum in Shropshire. He is now an author specialising in non-fiction books for children on a wide range of subjects. He lives in Cheshire with his wife and their two young children. Website: www.johnmalam.co.uk

Artists:
John Francis
Mark Bergin

Series Creator:

David Salariya was born in Dundee, Scotland. He established The Salariya Book Company in 1989. He has illustrated a wide range of books and has created many new series for publishers in the UK and overseas. He lives in Brighton with his wife, illustrator Shirley Willis, and their son.

Editor: Stephen Haynes

Editorial Assistant: Rob Walker

Picture Research: Mark Bergin

Photo Credits:

t=top, b=bottom

Dreamstime: 22
Fotolia: 7, 8, 13, 14, 17, 21, 25
iStockphoto: 12, 18, 19t
NHPA: 19b

Published in Great Britain in 2008 by Book House, an imprint of
The Salariya Book Company Ltd
25 Marlborough Place, Brighton BN1 1UB

SALARIYA

A catalogue record for this book is available from the British Library.

HB ISBN: 978-1-906370-50-3
PB ISBN: 978-1-906370-51-0

Printed in China

PAPER FROM
SUSTAINABLE
FORESTS

Visit our website at **www.salariya.com**
for *free* electronic versions of:
You Wouldn't Want to be an Egyptian Mummy!
You Wouldn't Want to be a Roman Gladiator!
Avoid Joining Shackleton's Polar Expedition!
Avoid Sailing on a 19th-Century Whaling Ship!

Large, round ears

Large head

High shoulders

Sloping back

Large teeth

Short, bushy tail

Short, spotted coat

Long legs

Large skull

Strong jaws with 32–34 teeth

4 toes

What do hyenas eat?

The main food of hyenas is meat. Some hyenas also eat fruit and vegetables, which give them moisture when water is scarce. Hyenas are **predators**. They hunt beetles, birds, hares, grasshoppers and termites. They will also tackle larger **mammals** such as gazelles, warthogs, wildebeests and zebras. Hyenas are also **scavengers**: they eat meat from the **carcasses** of animals killed by other predators. Aardwolves eat mostly termites.

Did You Know?

The only parts of an animal that a hyena cannot digest completely are the hair, hooves and horns. It swallows these, then coughs them up in a big **hairball**.

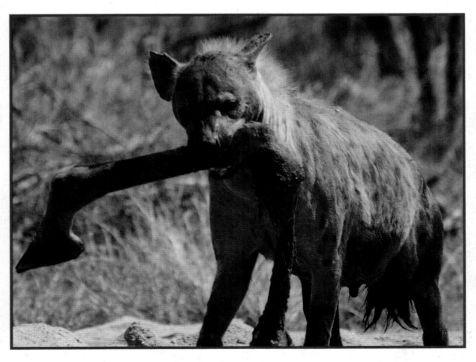

This is a spotted hyena. It eats more meat than any other hyena species. It rarely eats fruit or vegetables. Like the brown and the striped hyenas, the spotted hyena makes food **caches**. These are stores of meat hidden away in grassy thickets, and even underwater. The hyena visits its stores when it is hungry.

How do hyenas find food in the dark?

Hyenas are active at night. They have an excellent sense of smell, and sniff the air for signs of **carrion** (rotting meat). Their hearing is also very good, and they listen for **prey** moving in the dark.

Did You Know?

Hyenas have better hearing than humans. They hear calls made by hyenas that human ears cannot pick up. The calls let hyenas know where a carcass or other food has been found.

Spotted hyenas **forage** for food mainly in the low light of dusk and dawn. When they are scavenging, they use their keen senses of sight and smell to find carrion.

Spotted hyena

Water buffalo carcass

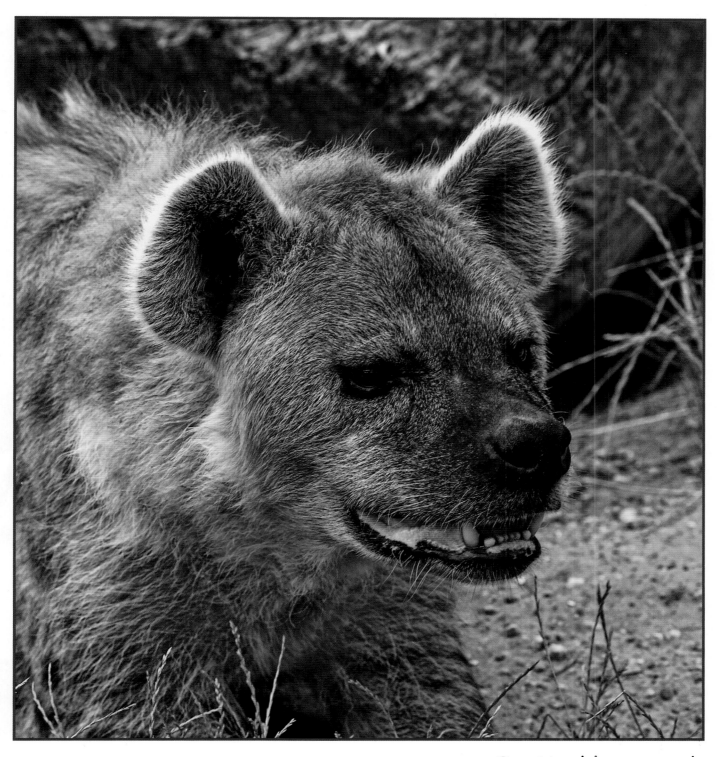

Spotted hyena cub

The spotted hyena is the only species active in the day as well as at night. All hyenas have good vision at night and in poor light. They have a special layer (called the **tapetum**) at the back of their eyes which magnifies light. In between their daily foraging times, hyenas are at rest.

How do hyenas kill their prey?

A pair of spotted hyenas approach a herd of zebras.

The zebras do not sense any danger because the hyenas are walking slowly, not rushing towards them.

Hyenas are skilful hunters. They work alone or in pairs or groups, searching for an animal to attack. Spotted hyenas will single out a prey animal from a group of animals. One hyena walks quickly up to the group, then breaks into a run. The group scatters and the fittest animals escape. The young and weak are left behind, and the hyena chooses which one to kill.

Spotted hyena

Hunting a zebra

An adult zebra will feed about twelve hyenas. They eat quickly, climbing over the carcass and wriggling under each other to get at it. The only part they will not touch is the rumen (part of the stomach). The zebra is eaten in about thirty minutes – bones and all!

When they are very close to the herd, the hyenas start to run. They single out a zebra and chase it. Other hyenas join in. The zebra soon becomes tired and slows down, and then the hyenas come right up to it.

Did You Know?

A hyena kills small prey by biting it around the neck or back, then shaking it until it is dead. This method of killing is known as a **death-shake**.

Zebra

They bite at the zebra's legs and pull its tail. The zebra falls to the ground, and the hyenas surround it. They bite into its soft belly, and within a few minutes the zebra is dead.

Do hyenas laugh?

Not really. The spotted hyena is one of Africa's noisiest animals. It has about eleven different calls, and one of them sounds like a giggle or a laugh. That's why its nickname is the 'laughing hyena'. It isn't really laughing – just making a noise that sounds like a laugh to us.

Spotted hyena 'laughing'

Whoops, giggles, yells, growls, grunts, groans, barks, whines, screams and squeals are some of the many noises made by spotted, brown and striped hyenas. The aardwolf is the quietest member of the hyena family, and only calls out when it gets into a fight.

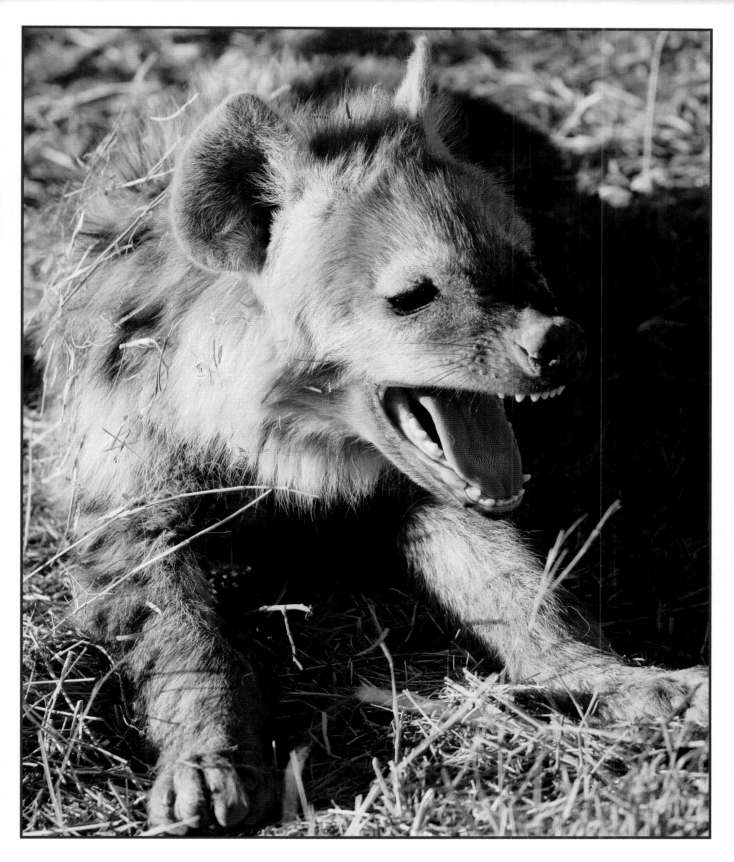

Young hyenas make squealing noises, which they can keep up for several minutes at a time. The squeals have two meanings. They can be a greeting call or a begging-for-food call. They are always made to an adult hyena.

How do hyenas say hello?

When two hyenas meet, they sniff each other's mouth, head and neck. Then they sniff the sides of their bodies, and their bottoms. This is a hyena greeting ceremony.

X-Ray Vision

Hold the next page up to the light to see what's inside the spotted hyena.

See what's inside

Spotted hyena cubs sniffing each other

Why do hyenas sniff?

Sniffing is a way of getting to know each other. Every hyena has its own smell which members of its group learn to recognise.

Even if they have only been apart for a few minutes, hyenas still greet each other by sniffing. The more junior (less important) hyena usually sniffs first. The senior (more important) hyena often yawns while it is being sniffed.

Spotted hyenas greeting

A spotted hyena usually gives birth to two cubs. Aardwolves, brown and striped hyenas will have three or four cubs. Mothers carry their babies for about three to four months before giving birth to them.

Twin cubs in the mother's body

Where do baby hyenas live?

Baby hyenas live in a **den**. The den may be a hole in the ground or it may be in a cave. The cubs' mother comes to the den several times a day to **suckle** them. After a few weeks the cubs are ready to venture outside the den.

Did You Know?

After a number of months, the hyena mother stops suckling her cubs. The cubs don't like this! They throw a **weaning** tantrum, circling their mother and whining.

A spotted hyena and her cubs. The mother raises the cubs by herself – the father has nothing to do with them.

Many cubs from different mothers live in the same den. It's messy, with food scraps and hairballs all around it.

What is a hyena clan?

Most hyenas live in family groups or **clans**. There can be as many as 100, or as few as ten, in a clan. Each clan has its own territory. Adults **scent-mark** the edges of their clan territory with an oily paste. They rub it onto grass stems. The scent warns hyenas from other clans to keep out.

Did You Know?

Hyenas make toilet places along the edges of their territory. It's another way of scent-marking the boundaries. The toilets are shared with the next clan.

A hyena family group

Did You Know?

Fresh hyena dung is green. When it dries out it turns white because it contains so much calcium from the bones eaten by the hyena.

As a hyena walks along the edge of its clan territory it rubs spots of scent onto the grass. It smells like soap. To the human nose, a hyena scent mark stays smelly for about 30 days. A hyena can probably smell it for longer.

Clan territories can cover very large areas. Hyenas will always defend their ground from strangers. If a hyena enters a neighbouring territory, a fight usually breaks out. A resident hyena will run up to it and bite and pull at its neck. The stranger doesn't bite back, but gives in and goes home.

19

Do hyenas have enemies?

Spotted hyenas have one natural enemy – the lion. Hyenas and lions prey on the same large mammals. They both hunt zebras and various species of antelope, such as wildebeests, topi, gazelles and impala. Competing for the same food can lead to fights, especially when hyenas try to rob lions of their kills.

Spotted hyenas approach a feeding lion. They walk shoulder to shoulder, which is a sign that they are on the attack. They are not afraid of the lion.

They try to frighten the lion away with growls and grunts. When it runs off, the hyenas will move in and steal its kill.

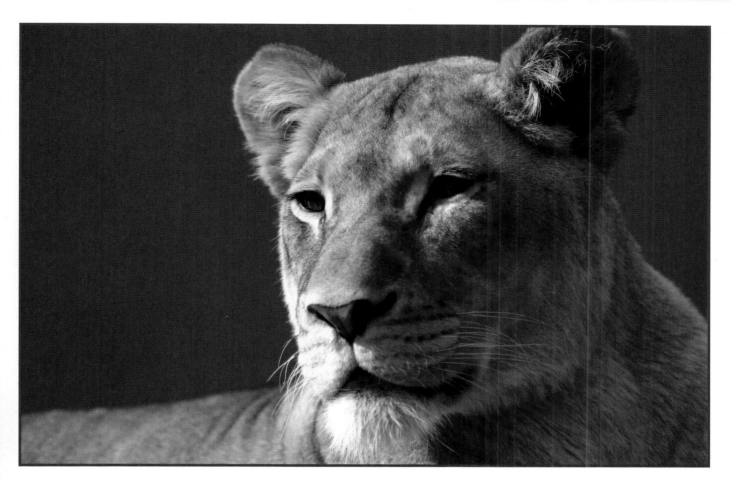

Lions, like hyenas, would sooner scavenge a free meal than spend time and energy in hunting one down.

The noisy calls of hyenas attract lions. If they find hyenas feeding, the lions will try to take the food from them.

Did You Know?

Lion mothers leave their cubs for many hours at a time. The cubs try to stay hidden, but if a hyena finds them it will grab one, take it away and eat it.

How fast can a hyena run?

Hyenas have three speeds: walking, trotting and running. Their walking speed is about 2–4 kph (1–2.5 mph), trotting is 8 kph (5 mph), and they can run flat out at 60 kph (37 mph). They can keep up their top speed only for short bursts before they feel tired and have to slow down.

Did You Know?

The spotted hyena can keep up a steady speed of 50 kph (30 mph) over many kilometres before catching its prey or giving up the chase.

Trotting along at the edge of a lake, this spotted hyena is hoping to catch a flamingo. When it trots, a hyena has a long, ambling stride.

Spotted hyenas running

When it runs fast, the lower parts of a hyena's legs appear to be loose-jointed. This is especially true of its back legs, which flop out to the side.

How far do hyenas travel?

In the search for food, the brown hyena travels the furthest. Every night it covers about 31 km (19 miles). The spotted hyena covers about 26 km (16 miles), and the striped hyena 20 km (12.5 miles).

Did You Know?

A wildebeest (a kind of antelope) has a top speed of about 80 kph (50 mph). That's faster than a hyena – but the wildebeest tires sooner than the hyena, so it eventually gets caught by the chasing predator.

Are hyenas endangered?

Many African mammals are **endangered**. They are at risk because their **habitats** are being destroyed, and because **poachers** hunt them. Hyenas are not likely to die out because there are quite a lot of them in the wild. However, they do face some threats to their lives.

The brown hyena is the rarest species of hyena. Because it sometimes attacks farm animals, farmers shoot it, poison it and trap it with snares. Even though only one **rogue** hyena might be responsible for the killing, some farmers believe every brown hyena is a danger to their livestock.

Spotter plane

The Brown Hyena Research Project in Namibia studies brown hyenas. Radio collars have been fitted to hyenas from different clans.

Radio receiver

Radio transmitter

The collars send out signals which allow the hyenas' movements to be tracked by scientists on the ground or in the air.

All hyenas are at risk from road vehicles – every year many are run over by cars and lorries. In Namibia, road signs (right) warn drivers if they are crossing hyena territory. They should watch out for hyenas wandering onto the road.

Hyenas are also at risk from hunters, who shoot them for fun. In Cameroon, Senegal and Côte d'Ivoire they are killed for meat, and in Burkina Faso, Mozambique and Tanzania parts of their bodies are used in traditional medicines.

In areas where locusts are a problem, poison is sprayed from planes. The poison can fall on hyenas and kill them as well as the locusts.

Brown hyena

Did You Know?

This is how many hyenas are thought to live in the wild in Africa:

Brown hyena	5,000–8,000
Striped hyena	5,000–14,000
Spotted hyena	more than 10,000
Aardwolf	not known

Who thinks hyenas are scary?

Traditional stories from Africa link hyenas with witches and bad luck. They're like some of the stories told about cats in Europe and North America. African **folk-tales** describe how witches turn into hyenas – so perhaps it's not surprising that some people find hyenas scary. Even though these are only made-up stories, people can be very superstitious about hyenas (and cats!).

In Sudan, in north Africa, a folk-tale describes hyenas as shape-shifters – part human, part animal. They are 'were-hyenas' that attack people at night.

Did You Know?

In Africa, some people believe that hyena whiskers, tails and ears have magical healing properties. They are used in traditional African medicines.

A folk-tale from Tanzania, in east Africa, claims that every witch has a hyena. According to this story, the witches ride their hyenas at night into the forest, where they gather together to boast about all the evil things they have done.

Hyena and Hare
A folk-tale from east Africa

Once upon a time, Hyena and Hare were hungry. They were so hungry they went to a village and offered to do a farmer's gardening in return for food. The farmer accepted their help, and gave them a pot of beans. It was enough to feed them both for one day.

Hyena and Hare made a fire. They poured water over the beans, put the pot on the fire, then left it to boil while they got on with their work in the farmer's garden.

Hyena's skin

By midday, the air was filled with the tasty smell of cooked beans. It was time to eat. Hyena said he needed to wash, and ran to a nearby stream. As soon as he was out of sight, he slipped off his skin, turned into a monster, and ran back. Hare got a terrible shock and fled, leaving all the beans for Hyena to eat.

After he had eaten, Hyena got dressed again in his own skin. When Hare came back, he found Hyena standing over the empty pot. Hare tried to explain what had happened, but Hyena accused Hare of eating the beans!

Hare tried to be brave. He said that if the beast came back the next day, he would shoot it with an arrow. Hyena took Hare's bow and scratched away some of the wood to make it weak.

Next day, the hyena-beast appeared again. Hare took aim, but the bow snapped where Hyena had weakened it. Hare ran for his life, and Hyena ate all the beans. Hare went hungry again.

By now, Hare was becoming suspicious. On the third day, he made a new bow and hid it in the grass. He said nothing to Hyena.

Sure enough, the hyena-beast came, but Hare was ready and shot it dead. He then saw that the 'monster' had been Hyena all along. As he ate his first meal in days, Hare remembered the saying: 'Greed does not pay.'

Hyena facts

Hyenas have bone-cracking teeth. Their bite is so powerful, they can break open bones as chunky as the thigh bone of a giraffe.

The spotted hyena is the tallest and heaviest hyena. It's about the size of a wolf. Females are about 86 cm (34 in) high and weigh 70 kg (11 st or 150 lb). Males are slightly smaller.

The aardwolf is the smallest hyena. It's about the size of a fox. Males and females are about 45 cm (17 in) high and weigh 10 kg (1½ st or 22 lb).

Hyenas may look like dogs, but their closest living relatives are mongooses.

Brown hyenas eat seal pups, which they catch along the coast of Namibia in southern Africa.

Hyenas do not make good pets. In Nigeria, west Africa, baby spotted hyenas are taken from their parents and kept as pets by people who want them as status symbols. When they become adults, these captive hyenas are sometimes killed because they are too difficult to look after.

Hyenas live for about twelve years in the wild.

A sleeping hyena curls up like a dog. It lies on its side and puts its muzzle on its paws.

In ancient times, dried white hyena dung was crushed to make a powder called *album graecum* ('Greek white'). It was used in medicine, and as a face powder.

The aardwolf tries to make itself appear bigger than it really is by raising its shaggy mane and tail.

When a hyena wants to show that it is inferior (junior) to another member of its clan, it crawls on its paws. It makes itself appear smaller than the hyena it is grovelling to.

At the town of Harar, Ethiopia, people put food out for spotted hyenas.

The Banda people of central Africa call the spotted hyena a *bongo*. To the Nyanja of Zambia it's a *fisi*, while the Gouragi of Ethiopia know it as a *woraba*.

Glossary

cache A hidden store of food.

carcass The body of a dead animal.

carnivore An animal that eats mostly meat.

carrion Dead and rotting flesh.

clan A large group of related animals.

death-shake A way of shaking an animal with enough force to kill it.

den The place where a group of animals lives or meets.

endangered Likely to die out.

folk-tale A traditional story which has been told for many years.

forage To go out looking for food.

habitat The place in the wild in which an animal usually lives.

hairball A mass of hair and other undigested body parts coughed up by a predator.

mammal A warm-blooded animal that feeds its young on mother's milk.

poacher A person who kills animals illegally.

predator An animal that hunts another animals for food.

prey An animal that is killed and eaten by a predator.

rogue An animal that has left its herd or pack and lives and hunts by itself.

savanna (or **savannah**) A habitat consisting of grassland which is dry for part of the year, with some trees or bushes.

scavenge To search for and eat dead meat and food scraps left by other animals.

scavenger An animal that scavenges.

scent mark A smelly patch left by an animal to mark its territory.

species A group of animals or plants that look alike, live in the same way, and produce young that do the same.

suckle To feed babies on mother's milk.

tapetum A reflecting layer at the back of the eye of certain animals, which helps them to see in low light.

weaning Teaching young mammals to eat solid food instead of mother's milk.

Index